Fantastic Cats



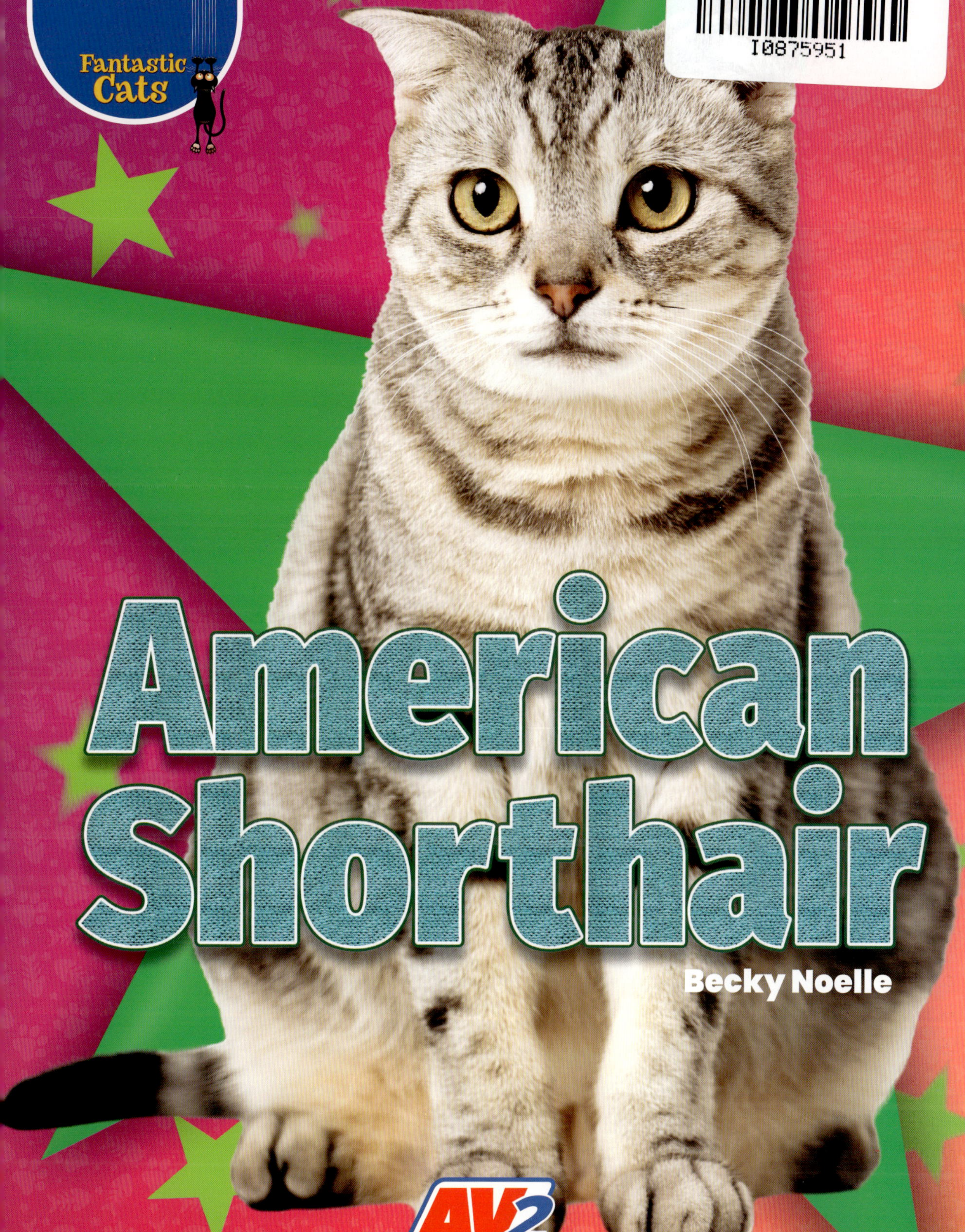

# American Shorthair

Becky Noelle

AV2
www.openlightbox.com

# American Shorthair

## Contents

# Name the Cat

Which cat is known for its easygoing personality?

Which cat used to be called the domestic shorthair?

Which cat was brought to North America to protect ships' food stores?

# The American Shorthair Cat!

# Meet the American Shorthair

American shorthairs are some of the most **adaptable** cats in the world. They are the perfect mix of friendly and independent. They enjoy playing with humans, but are also happy to play on their own. First known simply as shorthairs, these cats originally came from Europe. In the United States, people used them to develop a new **breed**. The breed was renamed the American shorthair.

American shorthairs are known to be healthy and **sturdy** cats. They have strong, medium- or large-sized bodies and they do not need much grooming. Their calm and easy nature makes American shorthairs a popular breed.

# The American Shorthair Breed

**American shorthairs** can live up to **20 years**.

**Silver tabby** is the **most common** American shorthair **color**.

In **2021**, American shorthairs were ranked the **eighth most popular** cat breed in the world.

# American Shorthair History

Shorthair cats have been around since **Ancient Roman** times. The Romans brought them to Great Britain. Many centuries later, shorthair cats traveled to North America on ships with settlers from Great Britain and other places in Europe. Since shorthairs are good hunters, their job on the ships was to protect the food stores from mice and rats. Once in the United States, they continued to use their hunting skills as farm cats. Soon, people started to call them domestic shorthairs.

People began to breed domestic shorthairs for their strong bodies, beautiful colors, and easy **temperament**. In 1906, the Cat Fanciers' Association (CFA), an important **pedigree registry**, recognized the domestic shorthair as one of its first official breeds. In 1966, domestic shorthairs were renamed American shorthairs to show that they were different from the shorthairs in Europe.

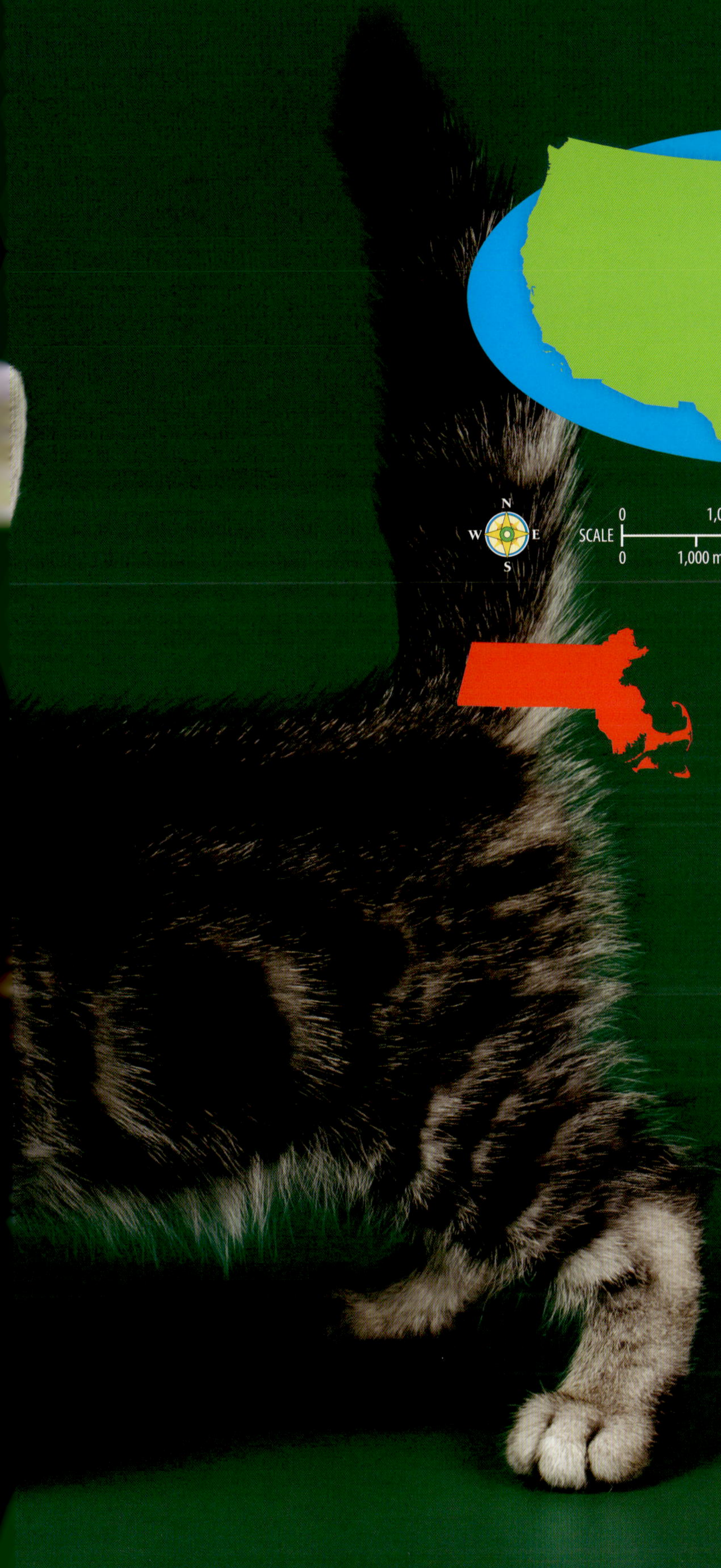

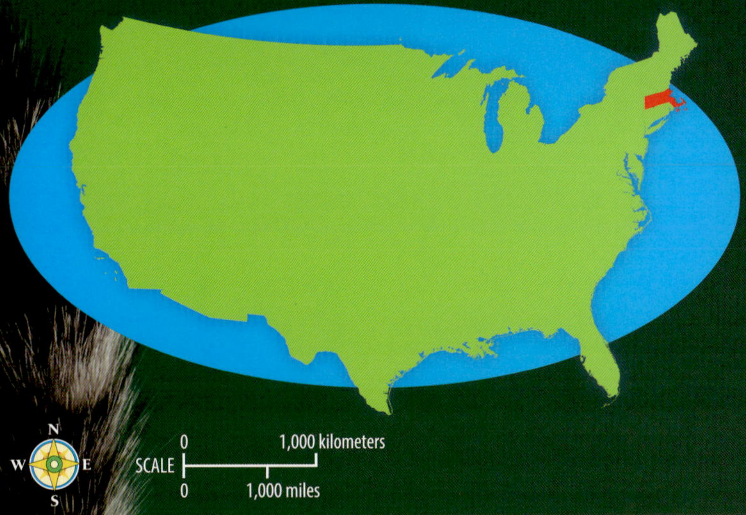



## Massachusetts

Some of the first shorthairs to come to the United States might have arrived on the *Mayflower*. This ship reached what is now Massachusetts in 1620, bringing families from England. The people who traveled on the *Mayflower* were known as Pilgrims. They established Plymouth, the first permanent colony in **New England**.

# Short Fur and Sturdy Bodies

American shorthairs come in many different colors and patterns. These colors include white, silver, black, brown, and red. American shorthair cats have some specific **traits** that distinguish them from other breeds.

**HEAD**

American shorthairs have square chins and medium-short **muzzles**. Their ears are rounded at the tip.

**BODY**

With solid shoulders, chests, and **hindquarters**, American shorthairs are strong and muscular.

## FUR

As their name indicates, American shorthairs have short fur. Their coat can be one solid color or a mix of colors.

## EYES

American shorthair eyes are medium to large and set far apart. They come in many colors, including blue, hazel, gold, and green.

## PAWS

The paws of an American shorthair have heavy pads with five toes on the front feet and four toes on the back feet.

# Easygoing Personalities

American shorthairs are known to be playful, good-natured, and **tolerant**. They get along well with children, dogs, and other pets. American shorthairs are also intelligent. This makes them very aware of their surroundings. They are interested in everything around them and often enjoy hunting insects and watching birds from the windowsill.

American shorthairs have sweet personalities. They do not demand attention and are less vocal than other breeds. These cats will communicate their needs with a quiet meow or with their facial expressions. American shorthairs like to sit in their owners' laps. However, they do not like to be picked up. They would rather choose when to be **affectionate**.

# Loving and Curious

American shorthairs love their families. They like being around humans and cuddling with them. Cats from this breed are also active and very playful. Their intelligence makes them easy to train. For instance, owners can train American shorthairs to play fetch.

Sometimes, curiosity can get American shorthairs into trouble. It is important to keep them entertained by giving them toys and opportunities to observe the world outside. With their strong hunting **instincts**, American shorthairs are especially interested in toys that they can pounce on like **prey**. They will also enjoy having a perch from which they can **ambush** toys and watch birds and squirrels outside.

# Make a Catnip Mouse

Hunting cats like American shorthairs need toys to stay active and engaged. Toys filled with catnip are especially liked by cats. Catnip is an herb in the mint family. Some cats are very sensitive to the smell of this plant. Toys filled with this herb can encourage a cat to play and exercise.

Catnip toys can be bought in a store. However, owners can also make catnip toys at home with common objects. A catnip mouse is an easy and fun toy to create at home. To make one, all that is needed is a child-sized sock, yarn or twine, and dried catnip. After filling the sock with the catnip, tie off the end with the twine or yarn. Cats will enjoy chasing the toy or simply sniffing the catnip inside it.

# Caring for Your American Shorthair

American shorthairs are easy to care for. With their short coats, they rarely need baths. They can keep their own fur clean. Owners only need to comb American shorthairs about once a week to remove loose hairs. Combing an American shorthair also helps prevent **hairballs** by stopping the cat from swallowing too much hair when grooming itself. American shorthairs shed the most during spring and fall. Owners may need to brush them more often during these seasons.

Owners should trim their American shorthair's nails twice a month. They should also brush their cat's teeth daily. Like other cats, American shorthairs should be checked regularly for signs of infection or injury.

# Cat Supplies

**Litter Box** All cats need a litter box. American shorthairs are medium to large cats, so they may need a slightly larger litter box than other cats.

**Water Fountain** Cats can sometimes get **dehydrated**. They often prefer drinking running water instead of water from a bowl.  A water fountain is a good way to help pet cats drink enough water.

**Toys** American shorthairs especially enjoy toys they can chase and catch such as toy mice, cat wands, or battery-powered toys that move.

**Perch** Being able to see the world outside keeps cats busy and out of trouble. A perch close to a window will provide American shorthairs with hours of entertainment.

# Healthy American Shorthairs

American shorthairs are healthy cats that can live for a long time. Their breed is not known to have any specific **genetic** problems. However, they still need to be checked regularly. Owners should bring their American shorthairs to the **veterinarian** at least once a year. If they have been bred with other types of cats, American shorthairs might still experience serious health conditions. For instance, an American shorthair with a Persian cat as a parent may get polycystic kidney disease. This is a dangerous condition that can cause a cat's kidneys to fail.

American shorthairs only need small portions of wet and dry food daily. They need food high in protein and low in carbohydrates. American shorthairs may become **overweight** if given the wrong type of food. A veterinarian can recommend the best food to keep cats healthy.

# Average Weight of Pet Cats

# If You Like American Shorthair Cats...

Many cats resemble the American shorthair in appearance or personality. If you like this breed, you may also enjoy owning one of the following cats.

## American Bobtail

Its tail makes the American bobtail unique. The tail is shorter than most cats' tails and will wag like a dog's. Like American shorthairs, American bobtails are intelligent and easygoing. They are good with children and other pets.

## American Wirehair

American wirehairs were bred from American shorthairs. The only difference between the two breeds is their coats. American wirehairs have a coat of hard hairs that poke out like wires. They need less grooming than American shorthairs. American wirehairs do best with as little grooming as possible.

## British Shorthair

American shorthairs are close relatives of the British shorthair. These breeds are similar in temperament and appearance. British shorthairs have short, thick coats and are known for being strong and healthy. However, British shorthairs do not like to sit on their owners' laps. They may cuddle beside their owner on the sofa instead.

## Exotic Shorthair

Exotic shorthairs are a mix of American shorthairs and Persian cats. They have short coats, but their bodies look like those of Persians. Exotic shorthairs have the easygoing and playful instincts of the American shorthair. Much like American shorthairs, exotic shorthairs have a sweet face with large, round eyes.

## Selkirk Rex

Like the American shorthair, the Selkirk rex is an easygoing and healthy breed. These cats are good with children and like to play with toys. The Selkirk rex's coat has a unique curly texture. Despite this, Selkirk rex cats do not need frequent brushing and are easy to care for.

# American Shorthair Quiz

**1**
Why were shorthair cats brought to North America?

**2**
What is the most common American shorthair color?

**3**
What kind of toys do American shorthairs like?

**4**
How long do American shorthairs live?

**5**
Which cat is similar to the American shorthair but has curly fur?

**6**
Where did shorthair cats originally come from?

**7**
How do American shorthairs communicate?

**8**
How often should owners comb their American shorthair's fur?

**Answers:**
**1.** To protect ships' food stores
**2.** Silver tabby **3.** Toys they can "hunt," such as toy mice, cat wands, or battery-powered toys
**4.** Up to 20 years **5.** Selkirk rex
**6.** Europe **7.** With quiet meows and their facial expressions
**8.** About once a week

# Key Words

**adaptable:** adjusts to changes easily
**affectionate:** showing love or care
**ambush:** attack by surprise
**Ancient Roman:** relating to an ancient civilization that developed around the city of Rome, Italy, and existed between the 8th century BC and the 5th century AD
**breed:** a group of animals with similar characteristics and family history
**dehydrated:** not having enough water in the body
**genetic:** when traits are passed down from parents to children
**hairballs:** balls of hair that may form inside a cat's stomach
**hindquarters:** the back legs of an animal
**instincts:** natural behaviors with which animals are born
**muzzles:** parts of animals' faces that stick out, including the mouth and nose
**New England:** the northeastern region of the United States that includes the states of Connecticut, Maine, Massachusetts, Rhode Island, and Vermont
**overweight:** weighing more than is healthy
**pedigree registry:** an organization in charge of certifying that individual animals belong to a specific breed
**prey:** animals that are hunted by other animals
**sturdy:** strong and tough
**temperament:** the way a person or an animal usually acts
**tolerant:** able to endure different treatments
**traits:** characteristics including physical appearance and personality
**veterinarian:** a doctor for animals

# Index

Published by Lightbox Learning Inc.
276 5th Avenue
Suite 704 #917
New York, NY 10001
Website: www.openlightbox.com



Library of Congress Cataloging-in-Publication Data available upon request.

ISBN: 978-1-7911-5615-2 (hardcover)
ISBN: 978-1-7911-5616-9 (softcover)
ISBN: 978-1-7911-5617-6 (multi-user eBook)

Printed in Guangzhou, China
1 2 3 4 5 6 7 8 9 0  27 26 25 24 23

042023
101122

Project Coordinator: Sara Cucini
Designer: Terry Paulhus
Layout: Jean Faye Marie Rodriguez

Photo Credits
Every reasonable effort has been made to trace ownership and to obtain permission to reprint copyright material. The publisher would be pleased to have any errors or omissions brought to its attention so that they may be corrected in subsequent printings. The publisher acknowledges Alamy, Getty Images, and Shutterstock as its primary image suppliers for this title.